THE GIFT
TO BE SIMPLE

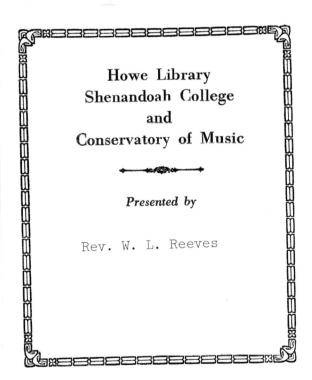

**Howe Library
Shenandoah College
and
Conservatory of Music**

Presented by

Rev. W. L. Reeves

OTHER BOOKS BY ROBERT PETERS

POETRY

Songs For a Son
Pioneers of Modern Poetry (with G. Hitchcock)
The Sow's Head and Other Poems
Byron Exhumed
Connections: In the English Lake District
Cool Zebras of Light
Bronchial Tangle, Heart System
Holy Cow: Parable Poems
Red Midnight Moon

PROSE

The Crowns of Apollo: Swinburne's
Principles of Literature and Art
The Letters of John Addington Symonds
(with Herbert Schueller)
Victorians on Literature and Art
America: The Diary of a Visit: Edmund Gosse

THE GIFT
TO BE SIMPLE

A Garland for Ann Lee

ROBERT PETERS

LIVERIGHT  NEW YORK

Published simultaneously in Canada
by George J. McLeod Limited, Toronto

Library of Congress Cataloging in Publication Data

Peters, Robert Louis, 1924–
  The gift to be simple.

  1. Lee, Ann, 1736–1784—Poetry. I. Title.
PS3531.E827G5 1975 811′.5′4 75–9974
ISBN 0–87140–609–8
ISBN 0–87140–103–7 pbk.

PRINTED IN THE UNITED STATES OF AMERICA

1 2 3 4 5 6 7 8 9 0

The author is glad to acknowledge the editors of the
following journals and magazines in which certain
of the poems in this book first appeared: *California
Poetry Quarterly, Granite, Poetry Now, Yankee,*
and *Invisible City.*

for Mother Ann Lee,
her gentleness in the face of vast persecutions and troubles,
and for her continuing presence here

THE GIFT TO BE SIMPLE

'Tis the gift to be simple, 'tis the gift to be free,
'Tis the gift to come down where we ought to be,
And when we find ourselves in the place just right,
'Twill be in the valley of love and delight.

When true simplicity is gain'd,
To bow and to bend we shan't be asham'd,
To turn, turn will be our delight,
Till by turning, turning we come round right.

'Tis the gift to be simple, 'tis the gift to be free,
'Tis the gift to come down where we ought to be,
And when we find ourselves in the place just right,
'Twill be in the valley of love and delight.

                                        SHAKER SONG

CONTENTS

PREFACE

This book presents in various poetic forms episodes from the early life of Mother Ann Lee, called by her followers the female Christ, who was born in Manchester, England, in 1736. She was the daughter of a blacksmith and as a girl worked for a hatter, cutting fur for hats. From earliest childhood she had numerous visions of angels and spirit-figures. Through close Quaker friends who had come under the influence of the French Camizard faith, Ann Lee founded the United Society of Believers in Christ's Second Coming—the Shakers, as the world came to call them. She believed that Christ's spirit possessed her female body, that she was the perfect instrument for completing Christ's incarnation— He had earlier appeared as a male, and now He appeared as a female.

The primary tenets of Shakerism were celibacy, complete communal ownership of property, equality of the sexes, and public confession of sins. Because of their beliefs and practices, the Shakers were often hounded by mobs, beaten, and persecuted. They were attacked numerous times during their settlement in America. Mother Ann died at the age of forty-eight as the result of beatings incurred during her two-year period of visitations in New England.

I have had to guess at much of Ann Lee's life. The details of her girlhood are lost to us except as they can be imagined. But her faith led to the visible establishment in America of nineteen Shaker communities, boasting some 5,500 members at their peak. Shaker farms were once far more productive than the World's farms; Shaker furniture is still among the most admired and sought-after of all furniture; their wisdom in treating diseases with herbs was legendary. Today, twelve Shaker women survive as the last practitioners of this impressive religion. Three women live in Canterbury, New Hampshire; the rest are in the village at Sabbathday Lake, Maine, where on August 8, 1974, the bicentennial of Mother Ann's arrival with her eight followers in New York Harbor was celebrated.

I am grateful to the University of California at Irvine for granting me a leave to write this book; to the MacDowell Colony, Peterborough, New Hampshire, for a fellowship during the fall of 1973, where the book was conceived and seen through the early drafts; and to the Yaddo Foundation, Saratoga Springs, New York, for a fellowship which I spent, in part, revising and finishing these poems.

A
IS FOR
ANN

Ann at twilight, Ann
at dawn, Ann with her

meager playthings on
the lawn, a stick doll

tucked into her pocket
a polished hen bone for

a locket, and on another
string a miniature tin dog

with a tin ball in his mouth.

One corner of the bedroom
where my sisters sleep is mine.
I keep it fine and tidy, scrub it
weekly, tack nothing
on the walls, allow no color
on the stones. There's one straw
pallet in the room, no
openings for light, a ledge
for a tallow candle.
I have a tiny chair with rockers
made by my brother as a gift
for me. The seat is wicker, the
rounds are oak. I sit for hours
rocking, staring at the flickering
candle on the brown shelf.
I see such splendid faces
looking down: angels, fairies, and
the face of Jesus, loving me.

THE HARE

I move the bough.
Sunlight slashes
the hare's green

swollen eye. A clump
of cornflowers near
his wet nose, a wild

shrub entangled in the
bough. He draws his leg
up and jerks it down

in a dying posture, stilled,
no moaning. Pus trickles
from the leg, small roaches

feeding. Flies on his belly,
black blood. Gently I draw him
from beneath the bough. The wound

is an animal slash, incisor.
I bring him to my face.
I carry him to water

cauterize the wound
with a twig, form a plaster
of deep-stream mud

and a leaf, tie it on
with strands of grass.
I feed him water from my

hand. I hold him, stroke him.
I walk to another tree,
place him on fresh grass and

bring a spruce bough close.
I pray and cross the air:
no beast shall find him here.

It's late. I run for supper.
I cross the field, then halt.
The spruce tree is aflame

with light, green fire hovers
over a tree, a ball. A voice
in a strange tongue, an angel's:
bless!

ANGEL SONG

A hart
roams the hills
above Manchester,
a roe in velvet
waits.
In a green tree a thrush
sings.

My spirit
wanders the hills
above Manchester.
My spirit is a roe,
my spirit is a thrush
at evening.
I ride clouds moving
out to sea.

CHILDREN'S SONG

She wears a hat upon
a poke, she is a skeleton.

He eats the matter from his
eyes, he is a simpleton.

He changes colors in the
flames, he's a chameleon.

He rides his horse throughout
the world, he is Napoleon.

CLAREMONT

Ann was astounded when
she saw her brothers
doff their clothes and then
chase Claremont through
the wheat and thistles.
Miss *C* was fearsome!

Caught, she fondled the
splendid laughing boys
as if they were unicorns
or spindles. Each one
she took by mouth
gesturing for Ann to
look and follow. It
would not hurt, she said,
and was not bestial.

Ann ran, heard Claremont
squeal and saw her weird
position: one brother pumped
betwixt her legs, another
breached her chest. At home
Ann sat beside the fire
unable to eat her dinner.

Gin and the king's men
again. The king's men again

and gin. The gin-soused woman
down the lane, the men near John

Lee's blacksmith shop again, and
gin, and the king's men begin.

Ann Lee in a chestnut tree,
aged ten: the gin-soused woman

and the king's men. The king's
men strip the gin-soused woman

and, again, she dances, her fat—
tubs of butter in the wind.

The king's men throw her down, begin.
The woman, the gin, the king's men.

I work for Thorp, Ltd., cutting fur
for hats, twelve hours daily,
from patterns devised by Mr. Thorpe
himself, who is successful, I am told

since London gentlemen buy all his
fine fur hats, of bold design, and
various shapes and sizes. For six
shillings per week, six days per week

I cut fur into shapes. The sewer
takes the pieces. I seldom see
my labors sewn. My eyes ache.
One mistake and Mr. Peck, the steward,
is enraged. I chant hymns

while I work, and think of
sunny fields. Today brought a
dear comfort: a lady gave me
a Bible.

A IS FOR ANN

A Garland of Shaker *ABC*s

A is for *Apse* and *Altar* and *Aisle*, as *A* is for
    Ant, Angel, Apple and *Ann.*

B is for *Benedict* the name of our cat, and *B*
    is for *Bangles* (worn especially by angels)
        and *B* is for *Bed, Behemoth,* and *Bat.*

C is for *Chores* that we do in the house
    and *C* is for *Clutter* and *Cobwebs* and *Cathay*
        and *C* is for *Coffin* and *Codfish* and *Cherries*
    and *C* is for *Cloak* as well as for *Caries.*

D is for *Diamonds* and jewels in the skies, and
    D is for *Damask,* the trapping of Heaven,
        and *D* is the *Dawn* for pleasing our eyes.

E is for *Eggs* (hen, thrush, and duck), and
    E is for *Eels* wriggling in muck,
        and *E* is for *Evil* counting his losses,
    and *E* is for *Elephant* wreathing his proboscis.

F is for bull*Frog* and *Female* and *Fool,* and *F*
    is for *Fairies* dancing on a pool when
        marsh*Fires* are *Flaming;* and last but not least
    F is for *Forge* and *Father* and *Fleece.*

G is for *Grouse,* the poacher's delight, and *G* is for *Grace*
    to be said at each meal, and for *Goose* and *Gravy* and
        Gravestone and *Grunt.*

H is for *Holly* and *Holy* and *Hands* twined in prayer, and
    H is for *Hawthorne* bush, *Health,* and *Angel Hair.*

I is for *Idols,* those we deplore, their names kept
    by the prophets in God's holy score; and *I* is
        for *Ice* that freezes our nose
    whenever *Injurious* cold winds blow.

J is for *Jay*, *Jesus*, *Jacob*, and *Jump*.

K is for *Kitten* asleep in the *Kitchen*, and for
 Kestrel aloft soaring over the *Kirk*.

L is for *Lion* with bees in his belly, and *L* is for
 Lion—fierce image of the *Lord*, and *L* is for
 Lion—protector of the *Lamb*.

M is for *Mother*, *Magpie*, and *Mad*, and for *Murder*
 and *Mastiff*, and *Marmot*, and *Maw*, and for
 Milk in the pail from the *Mooing* cow.

N is for *Nutting*, which we do in the fall, and
 N is for *Nightingale*, which we seldom see at all,
 and *N* is for *Near*, which the Lord is to thee.

O is for *Oven* where we bake our sweet bread, and *O*
 is for *Over*, as in the cow and the m*OO*n, and *O*
 is for *Open*, as our souls must be soon, and *O*
 is for *Oak* and *Oat* and *Oar*, and *O* is *Obey* the
 whirlwind's roar.

P is for *Parson* who looks like a *Parrot*
 when he *Preaches* damnation in the *Pulpit*
 on Sunday.

Q is for *Quince* and *Question* and *Quart*, and for
 Quarries for marble, and limestone, and *Quartz*.

R is for *Rook* in the graveyard so mournful, and *R* is
 for *Robins* and *Roses* and *Ruffians* and *Rout*.

S is for *Spinning* and *Sewing* fine *Seams*, and for
 Smithy and *Soldier* and *Swine* and for *Steam*.
 So, *Sit* here beside me, let's *Sing* a *Sweet Song*,
 for our lives are so *Short* and Eternity long.

T is for *Thrift* which we practice each hour, and
 T is for *Tidy* (so godlike and good), and *T*
 is for *Titmouse* and *Thimble* and *Throat*.

U is for *Unity*, for God, Ghost, and Son, and *U*

is for *Unicorn* that single-horned one. And *U*
is for *Unwell*, which is mother's state: she coughs
up blood at a frightening rate.

V is for *Violet*, and *V* is for *Vat*
where we make soap with lye, ashes, and fat; and
V is for *Vesper* that bright evening star, and
V is for *Venus* the lover of Mars.

W is for *Wilderness*, *Wisdom*, and *Wit;*
and *W* is for *Weaving*, and *Wayward*, and *Wax*
for the *Web* of the spider, the *Wave* on the sea, and the
Wattle on the cock.

X, as always, is for *Xerxes* the king. Try, if you can, to
find some other thing.

Y is for *Yeanling* dropped in the spring, and *Y* is for
Yellow, *Yokel*, and *Yert;* and *Y* is for *Your* heart and
Your soul and *Y O U.*

Z is for *Zeal*, *Zinc*, *Zero*, and *Zany*.
And if you don't like Ann's alphabet, now that it's down,
she'll call old *Zymurgy* up from his cave to
whirl you around.

CHRISTMAS EVE

Father is home. Mother is
sick abed, again with child.
I wash the table for our meal:
gruel, leeks, and a slice of pork
boiled, with hard bread splashed with
broth, and tea. Mother eats
only a morsel. She is so faint, so
broken. I sit alone on the warm
hearthstones, the broth-kettle
on the hob, the fire of hot wood
slabs (elm and oak) burned and fused
as a mass of red-hot forms. At last
a blue flame tongued from a stark
red orange center, a clash
of tints, striations, grooves
crumbling . . . I see devil
tongues! They run
streaming. The hairs on
my wrist singe and shrivel.
I feel no pain.
Lord Christ, still my demons!

BLUE
PALACES
OF ICE

SONG

Turn down the quilts, my darling,
turn down the warm quilts.
The candle whistles, elm branches
shake the window. Come,
turn down the warm quilts.

JEZEBEL

Painted Jezebel
wound her head in turbans,
sat high up in a window
to watch King Jehu
enter the city, to entice
and seduce him.

She had her wish, for he
saw her. "Throw her down!"
he ordered, imperious, on
his horse.

The king's men threw her
to the cobbled ground
beneath her window.
She struck parapets and
finials, spattered blood
on the walls, on the king's
men and horses, on the way down.

King Jehu trod her body
with his horse, mangling her.
He left her in the street,
entered the palace to drink
and eat, then ordered her
lifted up and buried:
she was a king's daughter.

They went to bury her,
found a skull, feet
and the palms of her hands.
The palace dogs had eaten
Jezebel. They shat her out
upon the fields of Jezreel.

ABRAHAM STANLEY

1

My husband doesn't intend
the pain.

Carnality is an incredible
thwarting of the spirit, of *my*
spirit.

I hardly allow myself to
feel tingling in my fingers
without shame. I avoid my
reflections in water, pewter, or tin.
The mind subdues, translates
the body's aches into the blaze
of God.

2

My gentle husband: his supple body
has the fragrance of oaks and maples.

It savors of forest ponds. His hairs
cling to his body. His back and thighs

are smooth pewter. I like the brush
and feel of his hair. But

when I see his gaze color with
lust and see his throat pulse

I pray for our guardian angel
to save us.

3

He strokes my hair (I can't dissuade
him). His hands close over

my breasts (I won't allow it, my breath
is in a well, my bones are

wet, nay, in the wet well of death). I
want to sing to God: Spirit, enter,
fasten our souls!

4

Abraham goes to the barn
attached to the house. The cow and

the sheep are fed and safe. The hens
are safe. I go to bed, bundle in, in

prayer, a life in my womb, the first,
a dear one, Abraham's, conceived in

sin. Let it be, I pray, a girl, a
gentle female for the work of the

Lord, in this world.

5

The bed shakes as he doffs his clothes.
He climbs in. I feel his hair. His

member pushes against my thighs.
I whimper. He raises my gown. Muscles

along my legs tighten and burn, my
buttocks are taut, my toes cramp. He

pries me apart. "Be quick," I plead,
"Be quick." I stifle moans in the pillow.

I am dry. The hurt! The hurt!
He strokes my neck, bites as he pumps

to a pitch. As he falls, there is a
luminous angel: his feet are curly
and he blows a horn. His hair
is silver, his wings are rainbow-

stained. He loves me! He loves me!
My angel loves me!

Blue
roses of ice glisten within the
great corridors and halls of
palaces.
Blue palaces of ice
glisten in Heaven.

I am faint,
I want peace, a place, Heavenly
Father, in a warm kingdom.

You have left a hole here in the floor
which your gift fills.

CHILD AND LAMB

Tonight, these flames
exude a cool wealth: round the end of
a log, fire drifts out as white
gauze, forms a fine spool encircling
a pole. Smoke drifts up: hair
taken by wind, drying the wood.
A child stirs in my womb.

The fire is loving, bound to
its host, it sighs, is soothing.
The central flames, in fives,
dancing, release sparks,
fragrance, in this room's air,
their tremblings and shakings
slough off all poison.
Jocund and kind, a lamb
is dancing.
A child stirs in my womb.

FEATHERS

Feathers have fallen from the sky
before. A bird knows that in light's

careful and harsh ambience his
feathers fall. Mite-and-lice-tired wings

pluck loose, or breastfeathers
wrenched by the wind loosen, painless

float as shadows to a path, a lake,
a pool. Each lost feather, each quill

is puffed aside, when we find them,
smaller, lost over in silence.

JOHN, ONE OF HER FOUR, IS DELIVERED

1

He lies with me. Thus far, he has not
found my nipple. He cries and

clenches his red fists. Dear Father,
may he live, a dimpled wizened self

with a soul moving towards Glory—
yes, the tiny fair heart jolted by

this cold air . . . I will call him
John.

2

Dusk. A single tallow candle
with a tin reflecting shield.

A fire in the hearth, subdued.
More wood, please. I can almost

reach the wood but am too weak to
grasp it. Perhaps his father

will come soon. I love your soft
hair, John. I love you, child.

3

I drift, dozing. I wake.
Something in the fire! A snake

brazen from the heat, with
warts on its face, a tongue

falling from its hairy mouth, the
tongue a pig's pizzle. The shoulders

have scales, arms protrude broken
bones. A netherself is hidden.

4

He blows fire, a faint roar of
his breath. Is he a sign, another?

For he appeared at Eban's birth.
Eban died coughing in my arms three days

later. Purge! Rinse! Scour! Scald!
Cut me! If my heart is rotting spirit-

meat, cut me! I taste, see, smell
Heaven! John, child, if you die

the fire-demon took you, he broke
your neck as you fell towards living!

Dear child, shake for light, shaking
is for light, for a harmony in your
tiny spent body and spent soul!

LAMENT FOR FOUR CHILDREN
DEAD IN INFANCY

w-oooo-aaaaa-aailll
w-oooo-aaaaa-aailll
w-oooo-aaaaa-illl
w-oooo-aaaaa-ailll

THE
CHILDREN

MAD SONG

A dead child's glee
is rain rotting
in a tree.

My bowels crawl with
lizards, skinks and toads,
green stench and fetid water.

A mother's sin
purloined their breaths!
O children, pray for me!
Please, let me in!

I sit in a road.
Fish wriggle toward me
in the dust. Crossed,
they lie at my feet.

I eat them raw,
heads, tails, entrails—all.
They are like cider, sweet.

Inside my belly, feet
tramp the fish into bits
of spirit-meat:
I have eaten my children!

ELEGY

Dead children's faces. Dead
children lying naked in the snow.

I walk up to them. Yes, I
touch John—he flees. I touch

the others, and they also flee.
I cannot succor them, they can-

not succor me. My spirit bleeds.
I see the imprints of their bodies

in the snow. The ice flows fast.
Green grass struck with miniature

white flowers sprout where each
child has been. I kneel to kiss

each spot but my lips press ice.
I don't know where to go!

I stand and, moaning,
pace that ground, until my husband

hears my sound. He strikes my face
to stop the fit. He leads me in,
warms me, and helps me go to bed.

RAT AND BAT

1

Golden plenteous gems of
earth and sea, the swinging

rat hath lost his tail
and where his nose grew

there are apples; his eyes
are cheese. In every manner

doth he wheeze and die,
whilst in the air a furry

bat's suspended wondering
why the rat's upended on

the wall. Who tacked him there?
It isn't fair.

2

The bat begins a
dismal lay of whiskers
gone to rot, of teeth
dissociate from the jaws,
of eyes that swell, and ache
and pop, and paws that turn
to instant mush and slop.

3

The moral of this little fable
(translate it, friends, if you are able).
is that the crumbs that tumble
from your table, or the rats
you hang upon your walls, each
has his solace in the warm red maw
of God.

ANN TO ABRAHAM

My sins are gigantic worms
with amethyst eyes and
scarlet heads flecked with
black. . . .

My infants, dead, are the
earth's four quarters.

My womb, too, has an equator,
zones, and weather vanes:

this explains my wasting away,
this explains my wished-for death.

My husband, there's nothing more to say.

A knot in a board is
the wet eye of an ox.

A knot on the wall, as I
stare, isn't there at all.

A knot in heaven is the eye
of a storm. Please, dear children,
come take me home.

I am transported
on a silken cloth, each
corner held by a
child. Trumpets blare.
An angel trembling
shakes before a throne.
His wings dazzle me. I
cannot see. A voice shouts
Jehovah! The cloth flies off.
The children clasp hands
in a circle. I float in
silver ether.

COME, COME, SHAKER LIGHT

THE WORLD

A choir of people burn
as they sing. A hand
with cramped fingers
bends over them. Their
words steam. Nothing is
titled, their words are
pentecostal. Their mouths
are eaten through above the
lips, blue gums, their heads
are turtles, chinless, leather
and green. No children
are seen.

The hand withdraws itself.
The choir trundles whiffles of
sound. Sand swirls over the
people. Bubbles of sand
where their heads were,
gases and exclamations,
the sun blazes
the hand levels everything.

GIFT SONG

Cricket and Cocoon and Caterpillar.
Sun, moon, and water.
Cocoon and Caterpillar and Cricket.
Moon, water, and sun.
Caterpillar and Cricket and Cocoon.
Water, sun, and moon.

James Wardley, a tailor, was a Quaker
from Bolton, Lancs. His wife Jane
met a pair of Camizards, in exile,
who preached Christ's Second Coming
as a *woman*.

With their gift of tongues
the Wardleys moved to Manchester,
converting some thirty citizens
including John Townley
who paid their bills.

The Wardleys found Ann Lee,
were struck by her piety,
invited her to join and
shake her soul free
from carnality. Ann joined,
became the Female Christ!

Hitherto Ann had been
their daughter; henceforth
she was their Mother.

A wife has her husband jailed
for shaking and neglecting
familial duties. Since he's rich
he's home soon, free—much sooner
than she thought he'd be. He
beats her and drags her through the
house, until she's as quiet as a mouse.
She joins the Believers.

SQUARES

A pattern of four sides as a dancing:
on one side a square of men across the
hall a square of women. Chanters to
the sides singing the beat, squaring
our jerking. We tremble keeping the
square. Angles intersect. We inter-
change sides, clap hands, reform our
squares, retire chanting.

March, believers, march, and step, believers,
step. Hallelujah to the Lamb! Hallelujah
to the Ghost! Christ is our Maker! Worship
Him!

SPIRIT-DANCE

As the red rose waves, I dance. As the violet
prays within its leaves, I pray. As the woodbine
twists, I cling to the oak of God: as the lily sleeps
on the water, in the soft lapping
of Eternity, on this troubled shore.

CHANT FOR A SQUARE DANCE

Scat to the Devil, and clap your hands.
Dance and sing before he plucks your eyes.
Devise, devise, good Lord, our sensing.
Scat to the Devil!

ROOTS AND BRANCHES

Origins of roots and branches, the
mysterious roots and branches of
blood and love. Now it is raining,
smoke is moisture.

Please enter. You are weaving.
I have spread fresh sheets and
a comforter worked from prayers,
filled with cedar.

The moon disperses the clouds,
the moon is tumescent, orange,
a glass moon, the mysterious roots
and branches of love.

GIFT SONG RECEIVED FROM AN ANGEL
BY A SHAKER IN A TRANCE

I have a little tambourine
that Jesus gave to me.
It's the prettiest tambourine
that ever you did see.

It shakes out delight
morning, noon, and night.
It shakes the Lord's power
and makes our spirits flower.

And with my golden trumpet
and my golden drum
I'll beat and pound and blow
the News till Kingdom Come.

HOMILY SONG

See the big frog sitting on a log.
"Kreech!" he says. He's king.
Can he be sure of everything?
He jumps into the slough.
You jump too.

GIFT SONG

Mother Ann's trumpet
was sent down from Heaven.
It glitters with stardust.
Its bell has a halo.

O dear Mother Ann, do
blow the sweet trumpet
and call us to merriment
singing and shaking and
clapping for thee.

The hemlock trees are violet.
Look: a knife blazes
in their midst, a jewelled shaft
and handle.
Come as water, Lord, come as smoke!
Come as a knife!

I walk through Toad Lane:
"The Lord is come!"
I shout. "Join me!"

A stone strikes my shoulder.
Another! another! I sing
louder, whirl, fall to my
knees and pray. Obscenities
fall as flowers, spittle as
radiant silk.

I rise and walk toward my
persecutors. My face glows.
They retreat. I have witnessed!
I shall witness again, until I die!

Ann is
a Jezebel, a
painted whore, and more.
Mobs pursue her,
shouting,
to her door.

PRISON

Measure the height, width
and breadth of this cell by cubits:
that ancient measure obtains!
Exactness is laudable and explains
what can't be doubted.

Yet, the dear fact is
I can't stand up in here.
This hole is limited by
brick and black stone.
I am alone.

PRAYER

The sixth hour of continual prayer
is the finest. The spirit
at last breathes, and silver
air tastes honey-sweet,
ethereal blood.

The seventh hour of continual prayer
numbs the knees, kills
ankle pain, the spirit swims
in its own golden air, and
quaffs the wine of rubies.

The eighth hour of continual prayer
is continuous blood, slowly
at first, from the fingers tearing
the arms, the blood transposed
into blood-light, blood, as the
wrists flow, solace *is* testimony,
is witness, a fair pain *is* peace!

Woe to this city.
Woe to their whips and
their stones, woe to their
swords, wheels, and spears.

They shall always be thralls, they shall
slaughter the doves taboring upon their
breasts, they shall smite their knees
together in bed, in fornication.

Glass fire shall consume their faces,
lions and dogs shall eat their young.
Their palaces, alehouses, shops,
forges and gardens shall burn.

And none shall look back, flames in
the fir trees shall be horribly shaken:
each persecutor shall be a torch running
to destruction.

Niter is the damp powder
adhering to the walls of

this dungeon. If it were
saltpeter it would explode

and blast a hole in this grim
wall, for a saint to enter

to lead me out, down a ladder,
free again, in the world of men.

If a mouse could talk to me now,
a whisker as a breath, a scurry

toward speech, and a fur-life,
here, warming a spot of cold flag-

stone, with a spoon of mouseblood
warming a slice of my fear, a slice
of my own dying.

JAMES WHITTAKER FEEDS MOTHER ANN THROUGH A PIPE STEM, AT MIDNIGHT

On the fourth day I hunger and thirst.
A hound barks without the jail.
I hear a child crying. A gray light
filters in. My back aches.
When I kneel to pray my shoulders touch
the wet brickstones of the cell walls
and the ceiling. I face the
keyhole, thinking of salvation, the
only way for air to enter, an orifice
for spirits to visit and sustain me.
I am startled to see the keyhole
darken. Something wriggled through!
A pipe stem!
I take it in my hand.
A fluid runs. I smell my
hand, the smell of milk and wine. I put the
pipe in my mouth and drink.
Strength soaks through me.
I praise the Lord, weeping.
I fall asleep on the icy stones.

THE PROPHETS VISIT ANN IN PRISON

Jonah rows toward me in a boat and says: "You,
too, are in the belly of a great fish, but the
sea is calm."

Micah comes filled with woe, desiring to taste
summer fruit: "Ann, feed thy people. Dwell
solitarily with them in the forest . . . not here,
in America."

Habakkuk sprouts golden horns from his hands and
pushes hot coals with his bare feet: "Drive asunder
these nations, Ann. Go forth. Strike the hostile
villages with staves of love, scatter whirlwinds
as you go."

Zephaniah stands with a cormorant on one shoulder, a
bittern on the other. He pronounces the restoration
of the lost, the persecuted, the prince of peace.

Zechariah holds a golden candlestick and bowl, and seven
lamps and seven pipes: "Ann, if you are angry with
shepherds, do not beat their goats. Pull the nails from
all houses deserving to fall down. Take courage from the
howling oaks of Bashan."

Malachi brings polluted bread, which he prays over
and bids me eat: "The wicked shall be stubble, and a
day shall come as hot as an oven. The wicked shall be
ashes under your feet."

Joel, dismayed, is filled with fear as he speaks, reviewing
the cycle of the awful worms of destruction:
> That which the palmerworm hath left
> hath the locust eaten; and that which
> the locust hath left hath the cankerworm
> eaten; and that which the cankerworm hath
> left hath the caterpillar eaten.

Amos, clothed as a shepherd, with a plumbline in his hand, is
last: "We shall not pass by you any more," he says, which
greatly unsettles me.

I have desired grapes
before the frost cleared
from the earth.

I have desired clusters
of blue grapes, the fruit
plumped with juice and

sweetness, dark. I have
desired grapes in this prison,
the singing of thorns against

me, the time of angels awash
in Lamb's blood, the time of
angels steeped in blood.

The best of my watchmen are
thorns brushed with ambergris,
they stab and pierce, seeking

uprightness and truth: I
blaspheme—my imprisoners say.
I do not keep the Sabbath Day

in the approved way. I preach
the crucifixion of spring
before the gates of summer

open. I desire grapes knowing
that the frost yet eats the bowels
of the mountains.

1

There lifted up my soul
a meadow mouse with eyes
a few weeks old, and hairs

still white from birth upon
his nose. My soul could hear
his happy rattle. He was so
small, and yet so strong and
gentle.

2

There sat down on my soul
a demon with three heads, a century old
and scales and claws and fetid breath.

He eructated, passed the foulest wind.
and laughed. My soul was flattened.
Its ears were deaf, its eyes were blind.

ANN'S VISION OF EDEN

1

A gigantic palm beside a
luscious apple tree. Before
me, as far as I can see

is a plain cut equally
by two intersecting
streams. Meadows,

flowers, fruit trees. Flames
to the north, smokeless, yes,
and to the east and south.

Elephants, camels, and deer
abound. Lions, oxen, pigs and
goats frisk and gambol around.

Birds and hens and other fowl.
An attar of roses, violets and
musk wafts over, delicious air.

2

A woman, nude, lithe and
blonde stops beneath the
apple tree. She's been

running. She doesn't see
me. My body, like a bird's,
wings down.

I hover, suspended
by a golden thread, over
the woman's beautiful head.

3

A man appears. He's young,
long-haired, with a short
fine beard. His member's hard—

I try to avert my eyes, but
can't. I'm even closer now,
an observant spirit, bland,

I feel the hot skin-glow of his
arms. The woman laughs
grotesquely. He shoves her gently

pushes her to the ground
beneath the apple tree. She
strokes her thighs lasciviously.

He bites her neck—an
obscene *munching* rather. She
sweats: her hair is drenched.

Her cheeks are flushed. Then
he pumps her. By stretching
her arms she kneads his buttocks

leaving welts. Locked, they roll,
changing positions. Ground-debris
clings to her back and legs.

A scarab beetle sucks sweat. Wasps.
A moth with a skull on its wing
lands on her shoulder.

The man rolls off, his rod grows
limp, his belly heaves. He sleeps.
Bird and beast have disappeared.

4

The woman rises, eats an apple
from the tree. The tree withers,
struck with blight, pronged,

suited for a desert. Bloated
toads with gossamer wings. A
blood-red cloth falls over the tree.
In the air a human skull set
above crossed bones floats.
A crane with a warshield round its

neck, numerous wailing miniature
humans, hiding their privates with
their hands, drift past, in grief
crossing their legs, welcoming
devils of fire who spirit them off.

The woman leaves the man, walks
to the split tree and urinates.
She pisseth standing. The blood

becomes a rivulet of maggots
on the ground, it sucks debris
and flows, surrounding the re-

cumbent man. He's covered now,
except for his nose which shows
him breathing. Steam rises from the
stream. The sky darkens. Wasps
cluster, swarm from the tree,
cover the woman's face and hair.

She blares. The sour hole
of her mouth. Her green teeth blister.
She screams. The wasps disappear.

A root drops from her
mouth, not a scrap of flesh
clings to her skull. She

runs in pain as the worms
eat her. She lies down
by the man, in blood, in

sexual congress. Linked,
they reach the Flaming Gate.
An angel bearing a sword

waits. "Doomed! Doomed!"
A wail of fire. A roar.
Clanging iron
defines the hideous air.[1]

---

[1]After this vision, Ann vows to remain celibate forever. Eventually,
her husband, Abraham, unable to live according to her strictures, is
driven out by the Believers. The origins of all evil are sexual.

RELEASE

1

An angel raised an arm
and brushed my madhouse cell

with a million stars.
Plants sprang all over the floor:

starflowers, moss, swallow-
wort, and dandelion.

Tapestries of grass clung to
the walls, blue air to the ceiling.

2

When the turnkey came to find
my corpse he found a woman

singing hymns, in the best of cheer.
James Whittaker, I later found,

had fed me through the keyhole.
The warden said, "A miracle!"

"The food of God is best," I said;
"and the Lord's wine is sweet. You can

eat his bread from the air. I
bless you for imprisoning me:

my spirit is more robust than my
body now, and free. Below this world

there is another; above this
there is a third. Only here

do we torture one another. Zion
is elsewhere. Zion is never near.
I shall realize a Zion there:

> *"He ariseth to shake*
> *terribly*
> *the earth."*

ANGUISH
UNTO DEATH

September is a month of
blood, of red moons,
seared, a misery. I
drive it out of myself
with a rod. Does the moon
on this first night of
his waning know
that he is in the south?

OLIVES

1

Olives must be
   as round as wheels, as
tough as calf-hide, as large as
   pippins.

2

One olive grows per olive tree.
   the single fruit drips oil
for bees to sip, a rare nectar.

The fruit is attached to the tree's
   top by vine-like tendons, so
powerful, so frail. A solid

olive seldom swings in the breeze.
   One olive
supplies a family with oil for a

month. Three olives, sold, can buy
   a dozen pairs of fine strong shoes,
fifty yeast cakes, ten yards of muslin,
   a hundred tallow candles.

3

I think I shall live to see
my own little olive tree.

The moon moves to avoid
Venus, tracking her. Venus
seeks a door into the moon
where she shall hide, become
the whore-brains
for the idiot-man sniggering
there, waning.

The fanciful end of our lusts
        is
to bedeck them with silver for
        the Lord.
To bedeck them
        transmutes them
into filaments of
        sapphire and spun gold.

The flesh is a bog,
it must be pressed dry.
The flesh is soaked cheese,
or it is a tree whose sweet
juices are deceptions of Satan.
To dessicate the flesh is to
lave the spirit with milk,
your body's fluid becomes
pure ichor.

A CYPRESS TWIG IS BEST

A two-inch splice
sharpened to a point.

Insert it
under the middle finger.

Tap the piece gently, praying
whilst tapping. Today I drove

The wood a good inch in:
there was no blood.

My aim is to insert the peg
under a fresh nail daily, until

all ten have been drained of
Satan's poisons. Be with me, Lord!

Place a small stool against
a wall, find an oak bough
three inches in diameter and of
your height, trim away the
knobs and branches, fix the
stick to the wall, anchor it
a foot higher than your head.
After an hour's prayer climb
on the stool, insert your
arms up behind and over the
oak rod, in the manner of your
Savior on the cross, kick the
stool away. Hang there praying
and denouncing lust until
your arms pass aching and your
hands swell and turn
blue. Hang there until you're
found beyond delirium, comatose.

Before the ecclesiastical authorities of this
town we accuse Ann Lee, of Toad Lane, Manchester, of the
following crimes:

1. *Blasphemy:* Ann Lee claims to be the incarnated
Christ, at his Second Coming.
2. *Breaking the Sabbath:* Ann Lee and her followers
disrupt the Sabbath with their public displays of
shaking, trembling, shouting, and wailing.
3. *Blasphemy:* Ann Lee claims celibacy as a way of
life for herself and her followers; this is in direct
contradiction to the Biblical injunction to be fruitful
and multiply.
4. *Sedition:* Ann Lee claims that in a vision she saw
the defeat of England at the hands of colonists
in the New World.
5. *Social Disruptions:* Ann Lee divides husband from
wife, children from parents, and friend from friend,
in the pursuit of her false religion.

We urge that the tribunal, composed of four ministers
of the established church, find Ann Lee guilty and,
in punishment, bore her tongue through with a hot iron!

Take five leather thongs.
When you are alone
in a cold room strip off
your clothing. Bind your
breasts tight,
allowing the thongs to cut
to the bleeding point.
Cover the area with a hot
(nearly burning) poultice
of cowdung and sand. Apply
this mixture by hand until
you are as flat as a wall in front.
Then lie on the floor, prone,
smearing mud and dung over
and up into your female
parts, until they are sealed.
Then lie spread, trembling,
praying, shaking
until you hallucinate, and
a vision comes.

Magistrates,
    I appear
under duress, coerced by my accusers,
to know the dire sentence of having
my tongue pierced with a hot iron.
    Look at me. I am short, inclined
to stoutness, with a woman's weakness.
    But my visions strengthen me.
They derive from my Heavenly Father
and in no sense contradict his teachings.
    I am gentle, my followers are
gentle. Our tremblings shake off
carnality, our public confessions give
us strength to live good lives. Our
    Father's ways are mysterious.
We follow his simple workings. Our cheer
is good, our dedication to this life
is good. . . .

Ann speaks in numerous tongues before the
magistrates, who are too impressed to sentence
her. Her accusers, however, are dissatisfied,
so force her and her eight followers to a pit,
intending to stone them to death. Only one
person is injured by a stone, the only Believer
in the pit who later defects. Ann's escape
is regarded as another of her miracles.

You see the sides of the pit
as amber set with emeralds,
narrow. There is a man
on the lip with a stone
in his hand, with stones in
his mouth, with stones
struck all over his body.

Next,
a stone flies,
exuding vapor, a handprint
in the air, tunnels in the sky
flailed from you, away from
the stone's trajectory.

The spinning of the stone:
you remember nothing.

"Stephen," you say.
Kneeling is a way of
shrinking the exposed
body.

Three more men at the lip
gesticulating.
Children in Sabbath dress
run to observe. Their mouths
are crammed with pebbles,
their mouths explode.
Child-obscenities
crumble, their pebbles flake
and touch not one of us.

Next
one of us is struck! Dust
cakes the blood on his face.

A shower of stones, motes
hovering, an angel with golden
feet and hands gathers them
as they near our backs and
faces, he gathers them
into his lap, into his raised
garment. The men on the lip
are fighting.

Stay, just as we are, stay
down here. They can't see us:
they are dust on the
tabernacle curtain—demon
spittle. They follow whirlwinds—the wind
and the waiting, the
waiting and the wand of God,
the wand and the opening
wings, the waves of air, the
weltering, the what, the
weir, the were! Praise the Lord!
We shall leave this place
for America.

CHANT RECEIVED IN A STRANGE TONGUE

ARE A ROKE! ARE A ROKE, O
INNA-NAFER, INNA-NAFER
HOLY. HOSTITTLE. HOLY, O
ARE A ROKE! ARE-A NAFER!
BLUT, BLUE-IN-ROKE, O NAFER
BLAKNITE, O-RONE-EO NAFER O
AS-AN CEN SHOW, AS-AN CEN
CHILL, AS-AN CHILL CEN ROKE-A
DEEM, ADEEM, ADEEM!

THE
CROSSING

Those departing Liverpool with Mother Ann Lee
on May 19, 1774, in the ship *Mariah*, commanded by
Captain Smith of New York, are:
1. Husband Abraham Stanley, a blacksmith, later to defect.
2. Brother William Lee, a blacksmith, later to die
   of a cracked skull sustained at the hands of a mob
   at Harvard, Massachusetts.
3. Niece Nancy Lee.
4. James Whittaker, a weaver, who had fed Mother Ann
   through a pipe when she was in prison, and who
   led the Shakers after her death.
5. John Hocknell, who supplied money for the group's
   passage and eventually bought land in Niskeyuna,
   New York, seven miles from Albany, for the first Shaker
   settlement.
6. Richard Hocknell, son of John.
7. James Shepherd.
8. Mary Partington.

The *Mariah* was a Snow, an old type of sailing ship
with a foremast, mainmast, and trisailmast, about
the size of the *Mayflower*. After a terrible storm—
the miraculous calming of which was credited to
Mother Ann, the *Mariah* docked in New York harbor
on August 6, 1774, some 78 days after it set out
from Liverpool.

The *Mariah* is slovenly:
her decks rough and oily,
spars, rigging and hull
flaked with rust and old
paint. The rigging sags.
The sailors walk and climb
like farmers or fishermen.
The captain walks the deck
with his head down, hunched.
He barks at the Believers
more than he does at the men.
The Believers ask for soap
and scrub the decks to have
better footing. They clean
the galley of odors. They
build traps and catch a
dozen rats in the hold. It is
not good to hear the rats scurry
at night. They are
becoming forward, they sit
on the Believers and wake them.

ON THE DEPORTMENT OF WOMEN ABOARD SHIP

1

A woman sailing the seas
must remain invisible,
below decks, where the
seamen will not chance to
see her; if she appears
where they're about
they'll fall off yardarms,
tangle themselves in hawsers,
and otherwise befoul the
operations of the ship.
"Ann Lee, our agreement is
that you stay below,
nor show thyself upon the decks."

2

Before we are at sea a week
I convince the captain that
neither my demeanor nor my dress
will induce lascivious thoughts
in the men, nor will they be
less efficient because of my
presence. Moreover, being a
woman of God, I say, and the
Female Christ, I shall bestir
the men to better efforts: "Their
bodies to you, Sir; their souls
to me!" The Captain acquiesces,
mutteringly.

Tonight
the sea's bones are easy,
a monster skeleton, a leviathan
catapulted, without crumbling.
The sea swings towards its mountains.
Ice-breath spreads over Heaven.

Tonight
my prayers slide through my flesh.
Their mouths burble sinew and blood,
they adhere to my bones, suffocatingly.
My nerves rip and shout,
without ice.

Water shot from the bow,
the hissing wake. Sails
ripping with wind. Sun.
The gulls left us today.
Throw nothing overboard
that can be eaten. We
have washed and beaten
our clothes. The sun
dries them. No one is
ill. Our courage is true,
the ship's course also.
But our enthuisasm in worship
angers the captain.

The passengers on board the *Mariah*

will henceforth

confine

their religious observances

entirely

to the hold

and

under no circumstances shall they

worship

on deck and in the open air in view

of the ship's crew.

/s/ CAPTAIN SMITH

The ship thrids
in troughs of waves.
The brightest star (it is
evening) plunges and rises.
Cascades of foam
break over the bow.

As the star weakens
we sink.
As the star brightens
we rise.

All of us, brothers and
sisters, are ill. Only
John Townley (he is seventy)
escapes lightly.
The plunging of
the ship's hulk
in a vicious rolling
induces misery.
But we shall improve,
shall acquire our
"sea legs," so
the captain says.
Praise the Lord!

THE OCEAN IS NEVER EASY

I am hurrying standing in one place.
  Unless I feel the earth . . .
  The ocean sweeps us up bitterly.
  We are knocked over, down, drowned.
I am standing in one place.
  Have we forgotten something?
  The ocean spews.
We were making good time, the sails
puff and blow. Never again shall
  wailing turn our eyes within, drill
  our brains, anything, everything, little:
(sailing through air and water) never
  a road, never a light in a cottage,
never a farm, never a rock, never an
  escaping horseman. Speak, weep,
    save us!

This morning a hand
spread itself
over the sea. Dawn.
And this hand's fingers
were chalcedony,
the knuckle bones
were porphyry.
The fingers, frozen,
could not calm the water
or shelter us:
chalcedony
knucklebones and fingers.

PROVISIONS

The six goats we brought for slaughter
and most of the hens (four
remain)
are today eaten. Henceforth we
shall ration ourselves
tightly
content to chew on dried saltbeef
and pork and sailor's sea
biscuits.
For a treat, upon a Sunday, we
shall eat biscuit pounded
fine,
mixed with salt beef cut up into
small pieces, with a few
potatoes
boiled together, and seasoned
with pepper. We are
amazed
to find our provisions so wasted
and suspect the crew of
thievery.

Bleached by seawater
our roots
every night on the deck
rattle against each other:
strands of glass
wishing to strike rock and
shatter.

These nights are moonless.

The leaf is not a leaf.
What is it?
Did it whistle down from
the mizzen,
dropped by a sailor?
The leaf is not a leaf.
The big dipper is wound
in vines, and a red leaf.
Is this leaf the spinnaker's?

A lantern is moving its light
over the water. Who goes there?
The lantern sinks in a valley of
water. It is gone. There is
singing. We cling to a bridge-
timber with a finger. A
lantern moves its light
over the water.

A fog as luminous as foil
drops near us
with its rotted rope and its
lashed cargo.
The ship settles
towards the fog
as if the ship nibbles
the edge of the fog's
limit.
A white note, a bird-gull spirit
drifts to
the side of the fog bank
sliced keen
on that side
at the ship's keel
white and open to the stars,
the squeal of the ship's
plunge.
Our eyes are red with
crystals,
the air is filled with
splinters.
The fog hangs like ice.
A breath whirls over
and consumes us.
What will happen will happen
too late.

A crack a flail
a graaak a creak
a thud a graaak
an ice-crack
a swale a scrape
a din a graaak a whush
a slap a krunch a
pummeling a
timber-smash

The ship spouts storm-water, it
thuds, wallowing, a shroud of
salt and water rent and gone
as soon as it is set
in preparation for another smash
of the same bulk and color.

The masts slosh through—
the illusion of a tent
dropped over the rearing ship.
Lanterns swing, their lights
held cold within their globes.
A ripping and tearing of sails.
The men have not had time
to lower or roll the sails.

A wail goes up: an immense slam
of water blocks the sky, a
large plank tears loose from
the ship's side. There is no
way to keep the ship from sinking.

The men pump hard. The bilge
is under water. Water rises
to the waists of the men. The
pumps are waterlogged. Pails
are useless.

"Curse the Believers!" shouts
the captain from his perch, the
handrail freezing the skin of
his fingers. "Satan, take them
to perdition! I should have
thrown them overboard as I
threatened!"
He's washed from the perch
to the lower deck.

"Pray, Captain," Ann Lee
urges, herself on her knees,
facing the storm. "He is
with us. He will send His
Spirit to save us." The
captain spits into the wind.
"We can save you," Ann declares.
"We can save your vessel."

The Believers join the sailors
at the pumps. They form a human
chain with pails. They chant
and sing. The water rises. A
school of fish is trapped
in the hold. The sailors clamber
to higher levels, entirely
abandon the pumps. Living quarters
are flooded. No one is dry.

Ann leaves the men. Again
on deck she kneels once more
to pray. She is lashed by sleet.
Rivers stream through her
clothes. The salt turns
sweet. Then: Ann is struck
by light. Calm as an
eye an angel suspends himself
near her. He flies to the masts
and touches each in turn.

The captain kneels beside Ann.
He sees the light as it poises
on each mast. A rift in the sky,
a full moon trailing stars!
On either side of the rift
black clouds roil and boil away.
Moonlight shed on the enraged
water lights the underside of
the clouds, a phosphoresence,
as bright as day!

A fresh thud shivers the ship.
The ship flounders and sinks as
if it will never rise again. It
re-emerges, it rocks softly, a
cradle calming itself. The
captain is amazed: the new wave
has beaten the loosened plank
back firmly into place: the ship
is saved!

The sailors man the pumps. The
hull is perfect, sealed tight.
No need for tar and oakum. The
captain calls it a miracle
wrought by Ann Lee! Henceforth
the Believers may worship freely
anywhere on the ship. The *Mariah*
is saved! Praise the Lord!

A hush follows a great violence:
the lashing seas run in
upon themselves,
the carved backs of enormous
waves
encompass and subdue all raging—
green, green as the eyes of
tigers.

We give over three hours
daily to our rituals, on
deck, within full view of
captain and crew. Our
visionary fits are frequent.
Half a dozen Believers see
Niskeyuna. They name
trees and clearings.
Sister Nancy has seen
the bottom of the Hudson River
as it nears New Zion.

ANN'S VISION OF A SHAKER WORLD

Come, life, Shaker life!
Come, life eternal!
> Ann, I am a community of white houses
> and buildings, three and four-storied,
> impeccably plain, with stairs to the
> sisters' and stairs to the brothers'
> lodgings. I face a hill crammed with
> orchards, and fields of wheat and
> vegetables and maize. Blossoms perfume
> the land.

Shake, shake out of me
all that is carnal.
> Ann, I am a hill, green and fertile
> with apple, cherry, plum, and pear
> trees. Grass covers me. Fat cattle
> browse beneath the trees. The air
> is filled with chanting angels, their
> melodies urge the finest fruit to
> grow, and the foraging cattle
> give the finest milk and cream. To
> walk here is to walk in the Spirit.

I'll take nimble steps,
I'll be a David
> Ann, I am a field of maize
> bordering a field of wheat. My
> ears are plump and sweet. The
> shiver of fall reaches the huge
> orange pumpkins and the meaty
> yellow squash.

I'll show Michael twice
how he behaved!
> Ann, I am a field of wheat
> in a flourishing valley. My

yield is greater per acre
than that of any of the World's
fields. Breezes
shake the heads of the ripe
wheat. Brothers with their
scythes are whistling and
singing as they cut neat
swathes through me. I am
bread, I am flour, I am cake.

Come, life Shaker life!
Come, life eternal!
Ann, I am a sawmill standing
on a foundation of granite
boulders. A stream flows through
me for cooling saws and floating
timbers. From me emerge the
truest planks for our buildings,
and for our furniture. My machines
are superbly honed, efficient, and
clean.

Shake, shake out of me
all that is carnal.
Ann, I am a spare, high room where
herbs and garden seeds are gathered,
processed, and packaged, and sent
throughout the World.

I'll take nimble steps,
I'll be a David
Ann, I am the long workroom where
chairs are made, and clocks
and buckles, buttons, pails, tubs
casks, barrels and churns, whips
and cheese hoops, baskets, seives
and oval boxes, pipes, and writing
pens. Here, too, clothes are cut
and sewn, bonnets and shoes designed,
and brooms and brushes.

I'll show Michael twice
how he behaved!

> Ann, I am the Church, rectangular, hip-
> roofed, two and a-half stories high,
> set back from the road, with a green
> lawn in front, an avenue of maples,
> each tree named after a young sister
> who must tend her tree until she dies.

I have two doors: on the left the
brethern enter, on the right the sisters.
My windows are plain: three windows between
each of the main doors, and a window set
in each facade, plus dormer windows. The
entrances face two gates, exactly opposite,
tied in with a white picket fence.

Inside, I boast a large hall paneled
with wood up to the sills, with beams
crossing the ceiling, and wooden pegs
all around the room for hanging chairs
out of the way, and for hats and cloaks.

I am the center,
I am the center of the Community.

ARRIVAL, NEW YORK HARBOR

Last night we anchored in
a fog. This morning
the fog lifted:
a miniscule town
scattered along the wide
curving harbor. Boats and
ships of every description
rocking at anchor.

My mind has dwelt perpetually
on the vast forests beyond
this harbor, where we must go.
The trees are wings waiting
to greet us. The trees are
thirsty for our arrival. All
around the Niskeyuna tract
angels have set flares. Zion
is a step away! Zion!